STANDING TALL
IN DEEP DOO-DOO

STANDING TALL
IN DEEP
DOO·DOO

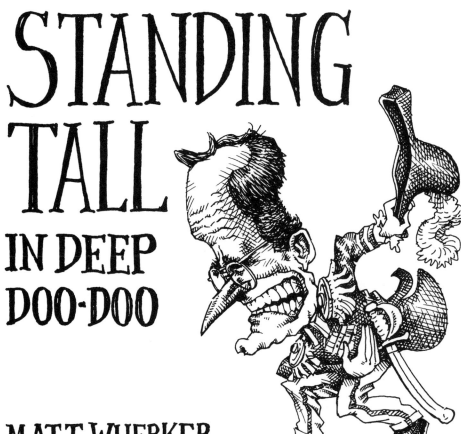

MATT WUERKER

THUNDER'S
MOUTH
PRESS
NEW YORK

Copyright © 1992 by Matt Wuerker
All rights reserved

First edition
First printing, 1992
Published by Thunder's Mouth Press
54 Greene Street, Suite 4S
New York, NY 10013

Library of Congress Cataloging-in-Publication Data

Wuerker, Matt, 1956–

    Standing tall in deep doo-doo, a cartoon chronicle of
campaign '92 and the Bush-Quayle years/Matt
Wuerker.—1st ed.
      p.   cm.
   ISBN 1-56025-037-2 (paper): $10.95
   1. Presidents—United States—Election—1992—
Caricatures and cartoons. 2. United States—Politics and
government—1989—Caricatures and cartoons. 3.
American wit and humor, Pictorial.
I. Title.
E884.W84 1992
973.928 '0207—dc20   92-5271
                                         CIP

Designed by Ed Hedemann
Manufactured in the United States of America

Distributed by Publishers Group West
4065 Hollis St., Emeryville, CA 94608
(800) 788-3123

These are the best of times and the worst of times. The world is going crazy and, especially in politics, lunacy reigns supreme. If you're a cartoonist, the grist is flowing into the mill; the fat is pouring into the fire; it's summertime and the satire is easy. In fact, for satirists, the ride hasn't been this fun since the "good old" days of Vietnam and Watergate. If we can just go along for the ride without slipping over the edge and becoming marginalized, cynical curmudgeons, then the trip promises to be pretty entertaining.

Owen, my three year old, seems well equipped for the ride. He's been confronting the lunacy of his world and he's particularly perplexed about how one deals with bullies. He has the usual reaction when knocked down by a bully—he wants to fight. Aside from my ethical questions about this approach, there's the simple fact that bullies tend to be a lot bigger than the people they're bullying. So, naturally, I jump in to try to help Owen navigate these muddy waters, explaining that we're confronted with bullies all our lives and that we have to find ways of dealing with them. Fighting rarely works, I tell him. It's much better to use our wits to outsmart them, to trick them by using our heads. So the next time Owen finds himself facing down a bully on the playground he remembers his father's sage advice not to use his fists. Instead, he uses his head—he butts the bully with it, right in the chest.

While Owen's bullies are smaller and more immediate than

the big-time bullies who pillage the economy and then beat up on welfare mothers for creating the recession, the nature of the confrontation is basically the same. While it's too bad that three year olds can't learn to hit back with satire (we're still working on that), maybe the rest of us should give head-butting a try. Given the state of the world, Owen's approach may make as much sense as anything. On the other hand, as long as politics has us knee deep in absurdities, it's not so difficult to seize the abounding ironies and rely on our wits.

Admit it—the world is mighty wacky. Dan Quayle is a heartbeat away from bravely leading us into the New World Order. Our intelligentsia are running around declaring that we have reached both the End of History and the apex of political evolution— we're the kings of the global jungle. At the same time, sensing new opportunities, the forces of reptilian nationalism—from Pat Robertson to militant mullahs, from David Duke to the ancient reactionary movements of Eastern Europe—are crawling out from under their rocks, getting facelifts, and learning how to use teleprompters and Stinger missiles. Meanwhile, back in the cradle of democracy, the "opposition" response to all this is to offer a choice between Jerry Brown and None of the Above.

In times like these, the cartoons had better be good.

—M.W.
1992

IT'S THE MORNING AFTER

M. WUERKER

MILITARY   CODEPENDENCY   COMPLEX

THE PRESIDENT OF THE UNITED STATES

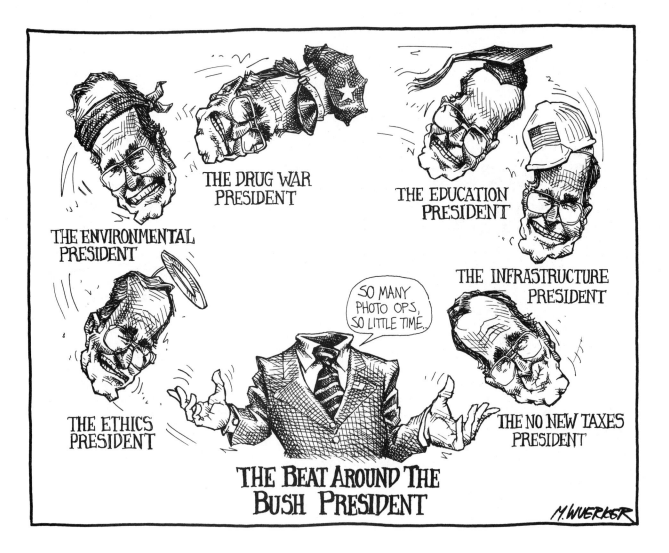

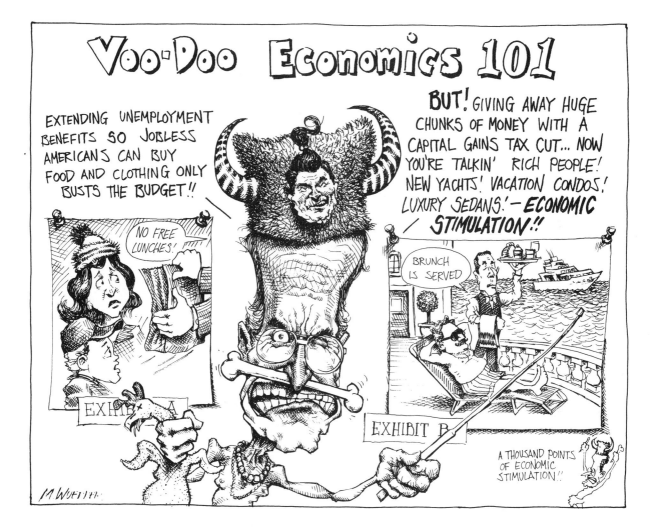

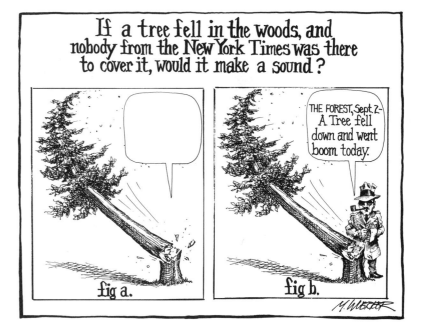

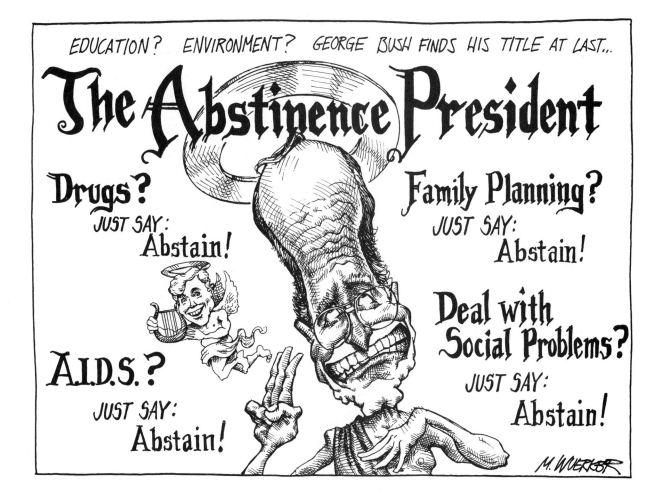

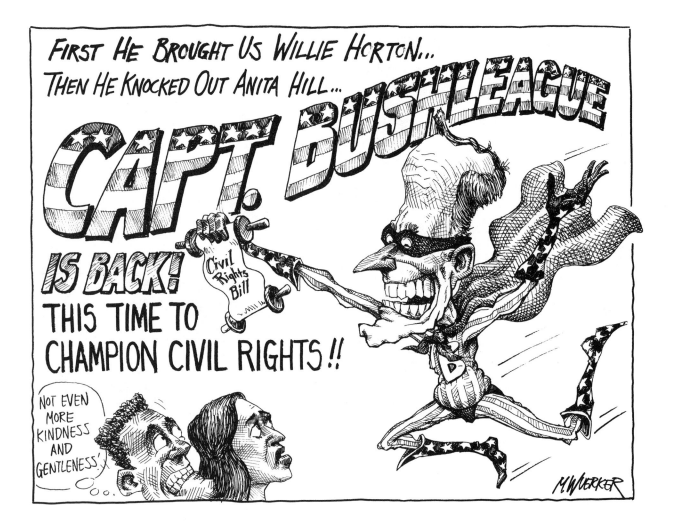

CRIMES AND MISDEMEANORS

Trickle-Down Journalism

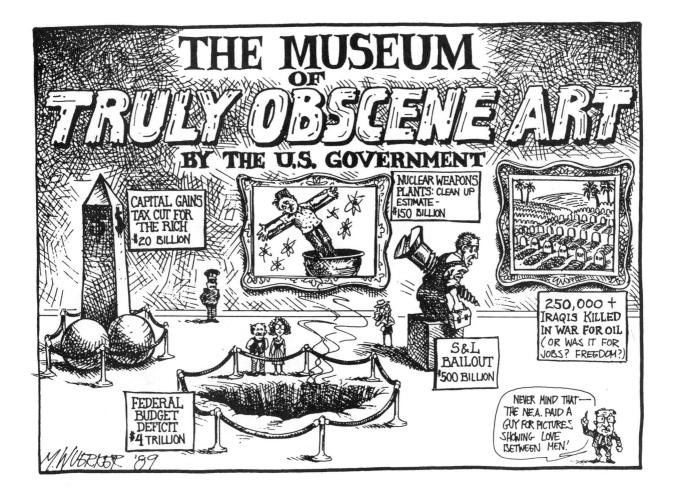

THE PRESIDENT
OF THE
WORLD

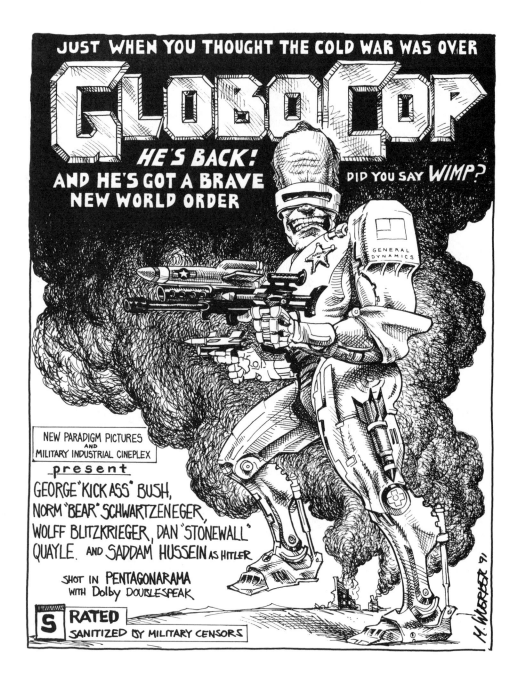

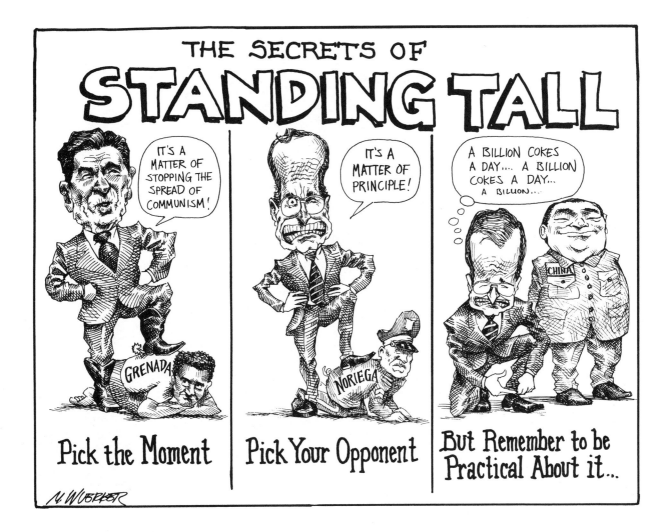

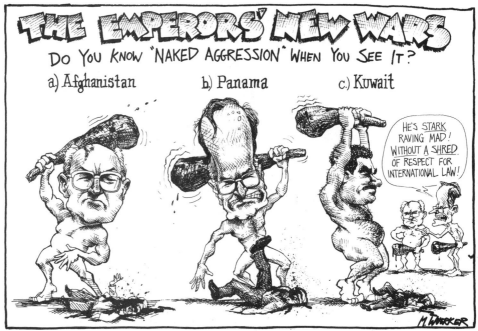

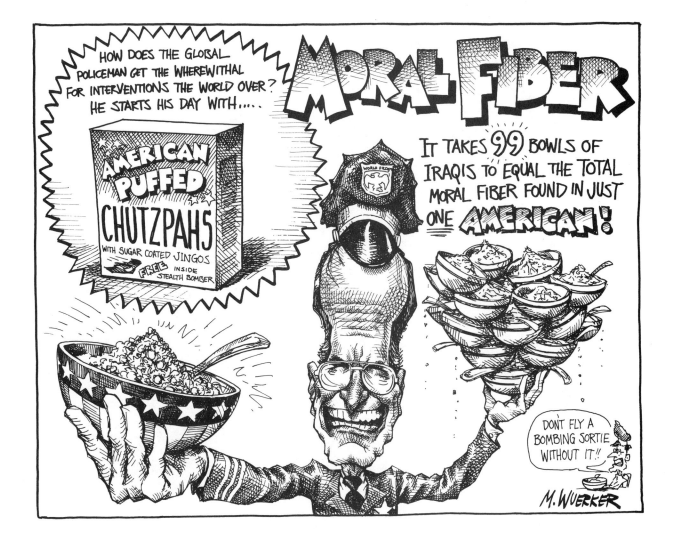

CAMPAIGN '92

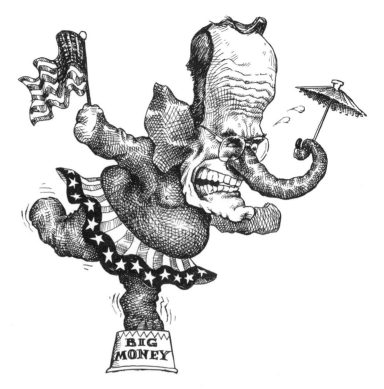

ANATOMY OF A NEOLIBERAL

REPUBLICANISH
NO CARD CARRYING MEMBER OF THE A.C.L.U. HERE. LIKES TO GET TOUGH ON WELFARE MOTHERS AND THE MENTALLY ILL ON DEATH ROW.

HAWKISH NOW RID OF THAT DARN DRAFT CARD, THINKS WAR'S SWELL.

PRO-WOMANISH
BELIEVES IN THE J.F.K. SCHOOL OF AFFIRMATIVE ACTION, ESPECIALLY WITH BLONDES.

PRO-BUSINESSISH
KNOWS MORE CAMPAIGN CONTRIBUTIONS ARE TO BE HAD IN THE BOARD ROOM THAN THE SHOP FLOOR

ENVIRONMENTALISH
LIKES THE LOOK, BUT ONLY AS LONG AS IT DOESN'T GET IN THE WAY OF BUSINESS.

CLINTON

M. WUERKER

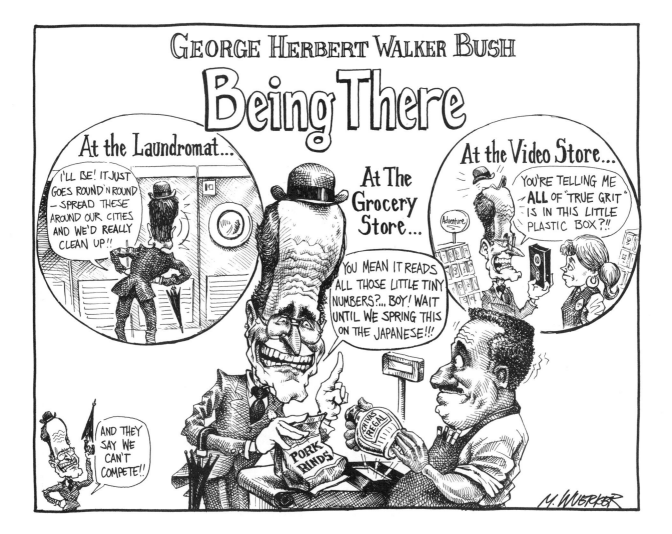

THE EMPEROR'S NEW WAR MACHINE

the silence of the lambs

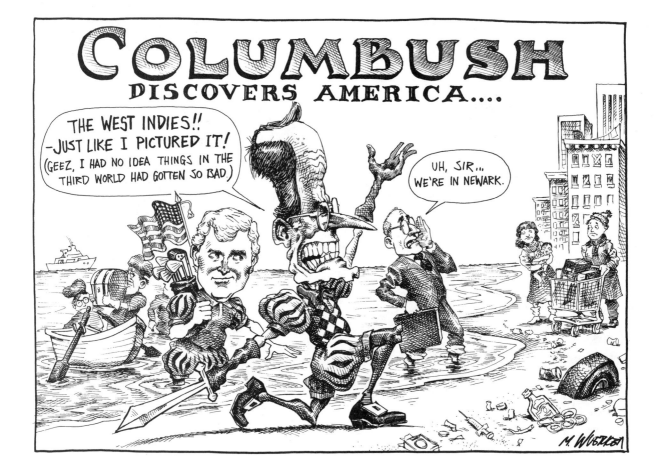

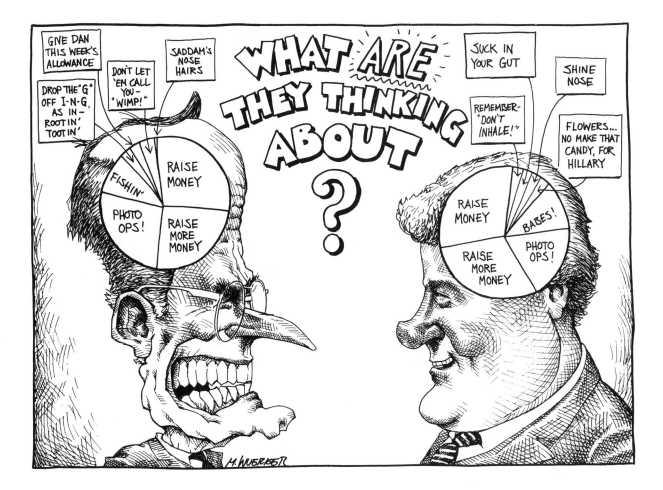

WHICH ELVIS WILL GET THE STAMP OF APPROVAL?

THE LANKY IDEALISTIC REBEL

THE JADED WORLDLY SHOWMAN